ENERGY FILES

WATER

Maltby Manor Academy

MALTBY MANOR ACADEM
DAVY DRIVE
MALTBY
ROTHERHAM S66 8II
Tel: 01709 8133

ENERGY FILES – WATER
was produced by

David West 👫 Children's Books
7 Princeton Court
55 Felsham Road
London SW15 1AZ

Editor: James Pickering
Picture Research: Carrie Haines

First published in Great Britain in 2002 by
Heinemann Library, Halley Court, Jordan Hill,
Oxford OX2 8EJ, a division of Reed Educational
and Professional Publishing Limited.

OXFORD MELBOURNE AUCKLAND
JOHANNESBURG BLANTYRE GABORONE
IBADAN PORTSMOUTH (NH) USA CHICAGO

Copyright © 2002 David West Children's Books

06 05 04 03 02
10 9 8 7 6 5 4 3 2 1

ISBN 0 431 15574 7 (HB)
ISBN 0 431 15581 X (PB)

British Library Cataloguing in Publication Data

Parker, Steve, 1952 -
Water. - (Energy files)
1. Water-power - Juvenile literature
I. Title
333.9'14

Printed and bound in Italy

PHOTO CREDITS :
Abbreviations: t-top, m-middle, b-bottom, r-right,
l-left, c-centre.

Front cover all - Corbis Images. 3, 4t, 5tr & 15br,
5b & 26br, 6bl, ml, mr & br, 7tl, tr, & bl, 8tr, 9tl
& m, 10-11t, 12bl, 13tl & br, 15ml & br, 16bl,
17tl & br, 20tr, 22br - Corbis Images. 4b, 18-19t -
Popperfoto/Reuters. 6b - Cavendish Laboratory,
University of Cambridge. 9br - Sally
Morgan/Ecoscene. 10-11b, 12-13b, 14tr, 18mr,
21br, 29tr - Robert Harding Picture Library. 11tr -
(Michael Jenner), 11ml, 23tr (Walter Rawlings),
11br (Pierre Tetrel), 13mr (M.H. Black), 19br, 20-
21 (G. Corrigan), 21tr (Simon Harris), 22tl
(I. Griffiths), 22tr (Paolo Koch), 22-23 (Robert
Francis), 28-29 (Louis Salou) - Robert Harding
Picture Library. 15tr, 20bl - M. Watson/Ardea
London Ltd.

*An explanation of difficult words can be
found in the glossary on page 31.*

ENERGY FILES

WATER

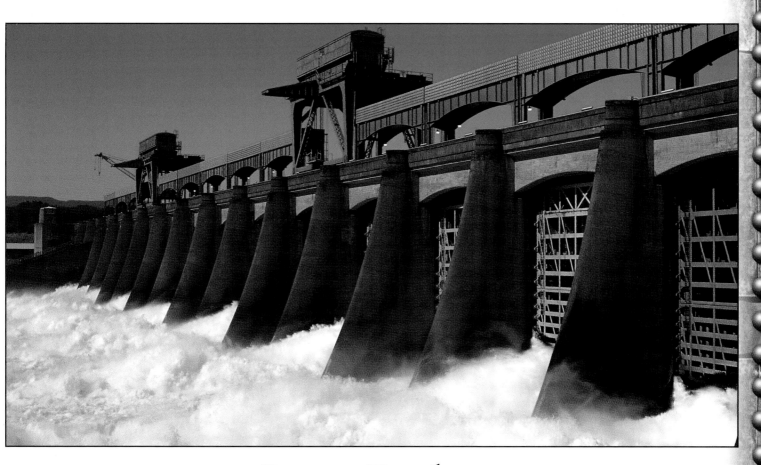

Steve Parker

Heinemann LIBRARY

CONTENTS

The pent-up power of water behind a dam can be released as needed. The trapped water is also useful for farming, sailing and leisure pursuits.

We can control where water flows, using channels, dams and barriers. But it is a costly process, consuming much energy and many resources.

INTRODUCTION

Water is everywhere – in streams, rivers, lakes and seas, in the sky as clouds and rain, in foods and drinks, and in our taps, tubs and washing machines. Even our own bodies are two-thirds water. This amazing substance is vital for all forms of life. But water is also a vital source of energy. Moving water can be harnessed to work machinery and generate electricity. In the future, splitting apart water may give us a new form of energy.

Crashing waves show the massive amounts of energy in moving water. They pound cliffs and smash solid rock.

In a hydroelectric power station, water rushes through rows of giant turbines, which spin the generators to make electricity.

WHAT IS WATER?

H₂O

Pure water has no smell, no taste and no colour. It's usually a liquid, which means it can change shape and flow. But water is not always a liquid ...

WHEN WATER GOES HARD

If water becomes very cold, it turns into a hard solid. We say that it 'freezes into ice'. If water gets very hot it turns into a gas – it 'boils into steam'. So water can be solid, liquid or gas, depending on temperature. Also, liquid water is an amazing solvent. This means other substances can dissolve, or melt, into it. Stir sugar or salt into water and they dissolve. They seem to disappear – but we can still taste them.

Long ago, people thought that everything in the world was made of four single, pure substances – earth, air, fire and water. These were known as the 'four elements'. But in 1784, scientist Henry Cavendish showed that water contained two even simpler substances, hydrogen and oxygen.

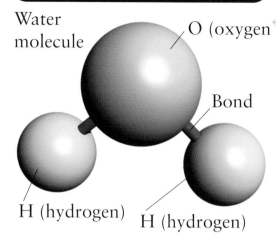

Water molecule
O (oxygen)
Bond
H (hydrogen)   H (hydrogen)

Like all substances, water is made of tiny pieces called atoms. Two hydrogen atoms (H_2) and one oxygen atom (O) join by bonds to form one molecule of water. In one drop of water, there are 10 billion billion molecules of water.

Henry Cavendish, 1731–1810.

EARTH

AIR

FIRE   *WATER*

100°C (boiling)

100
90
80
70
60
50
40
30
20
10
0

Steam from a hot spring is a mix of tiny water droplets and boiling-hot water vapour.

Icicles, snow, hail and frost are all forms of solid water that occur in nature.

0°C (freezing)

Green ISSUES

Our world is heating up very slowly, due to pollution and the waste gases we pump into the air. Global warming melts the giant ice sheets at the North and South Poles. As they change into liquid water, the sea level will rise. The extra water will flood islands and coasts.

Ice sheets melting in Antarctica.

THE CELSIUS SCALE

Water's changing form, or state, is so important that it has become the basis of our temperature scale, Celsius. As water cools, the temperature at which it changes into ice is called freezing point, or 0°C on the thermometer. The temperature at which it heats into steam is known as 100°C or boiling point.

GO WITH THE FLOW

Liquid water flows very easily, changing shape to fill any container. It also spreads out over a flat surface – as we know when we spill a drink. This ability of liquid water to flow is very important. It means water moves – and anything that moves has energy.

Water is always coming and going. Rain falls and soaks into the ground. Ponds fill in winter and dry up in summer. Puddles vanish in hot sunshine. Water flows out of the tap and away down the plughole.

THE SAME WATER

But 'old' water does not get destroyed, while 'new' water gets made. The same water goes round and round. A puddle dries because its water changes into invisible water vapour, that floats into the air. This rises, cools to form a cloud, falls as rain – and fills the puddle again.

Water flows fastest down cliffs, as a waterfall. This water has lots of energy.

The Sun powers the water cycle. Its heat evaporates liquid water into vapour. This rises and cools, and condenses – turns back into liquid water.

Rivers are grooves that carry rain and ground water down to lakes and seas.

Water on water – tiny floating drops form clouds above the sea's water.

Sea evaporates skywards, and rivers run into the sea.

Trees give off water vapour through the leaves.

SUN POWER

Water is constantly changing from liquid to vapour and floating up into the air. We call it 'drying'. The heat for this to happen comes from the Sun (or our tumble-driers and fires). It's the Sun's warmth that makes water move, and this is what gives it energy.

Water freezes on cold mountain tops.

Rain falls when the drops in a cloud become too heavy to float.

Ground water is water that soaks into soil and rocks. It flows slowly downhill like an underground river.

Water in lakes looks still, but it is slowly moving.

Lakes send water vapour into the air as more water seeps in.

Green ISSUES

In many parts of the world, especially tropical rainforests, trees are cut down at a terrifying rate. Without their roots to hold the soil and suck up rain water, the rain washes the soil into rivers. Plants can no longer grow, rivers clog with mud and silt, and the area is destroyed.

Deforestation destruction.

UP, DOWN AND ALONG

The Sun's heat slowly changes liquid water in rivers, lakes and seas, into warm water vapour. This rises and blows in the wind. High up, air is colder. The vapour turns back into liquid water, as tiny floating drops in clouds. The drops clump together, get heavier and fall as rain. This fills rivers, lakes and seas. The Sun's heat …

MOVING WATER

Dip your hand in a stream, and you can feel the power of running water. For over two thousand years, people have harnessed this energy to drive machines, using waterwheels.

ANCIENT IDEA

The first waterwheels turned in the Middle East, ancient Rome and China. They spread across Europe and Asia and by a thousand years ago, they were very common. In AD 1087, England had over 5,000.

WATERWHEEL DESIGNS

Undershot waterwheel

The waterwheel is usually two wheels with paddles or blades around the rim. In the undershot design, the water goes past the base of the wheel. In the overshot version, it pours on to the top. This needs a greater drop in water height.

Direction of water flow

Turning wheel provides power for machinery.

Factory wheel on a purpose-made stream, the race.

WATERWHEEL LIMITS

Moving water energy is 'free', provided by nature. In the 1700s, before steam power, water power kick-started the Industrial Revolution. But it has limits. Water flow must be reliable all year – a fast flood will smash the wheel, while a drought leaves it idle. Other machines like millstones, to grind wheat, or weaving looms, to make cloth, must also be next to the stream. This means factories need to be in hilly, wet places with plenty of running water.

Ancient TECHNOLOGY

Waterwheels were made of wood, so few ancient ones survive. Their water flow often came from specially built channels or pipes, bringing the energy to where it was needed.

Giant waterwheel, Syria.

RAISING WATER

The waterlift is as old as the waterwheel. A source of energy turns the wheel, or a curved ramp called the Archimedes screw, to raise or move water. This is especially useful for watering fields or providing a village drinking supply.

In the waterlift, energy from animals or machines turns a wheel (above) or a screw (right). This raises water from a well or channel.

Direction of rotation

Handle turned

Water is drawn up.

Running water has so much energy, it is difficult to stop. A dam is a thick, strong wall across a stream or river, to hold back the flow. The pent-up water is, in effect, stored energy.

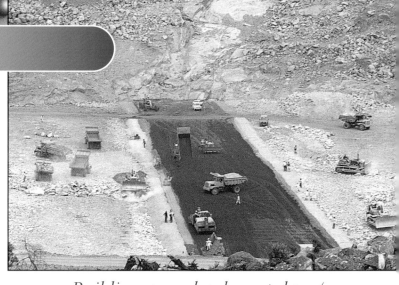

Building an embankment dam (see below) in Swaziland, Africa.

WHY BUILD DAMS?

Giant dams are some of the biggest structures ever built. Why go to so much effort? Modern dams have many uses. Once the water is under control it can be used as an energy source, also to water crops and farm animals, for human use, to prevent droughts and floods – and for fun!

INSIDE A DAM

The embankment dam is a simple type of gravity dam. It relies on its great weight, rather than a specialized shape, to hold back the water. Its construction can be adapted to local building materials and it needs little special machinery. The waterproof clay core prevents slow seepage.

Lake Nasser behind the Aswan High Dam, across the Nile in Egypt, is over 500 km long.

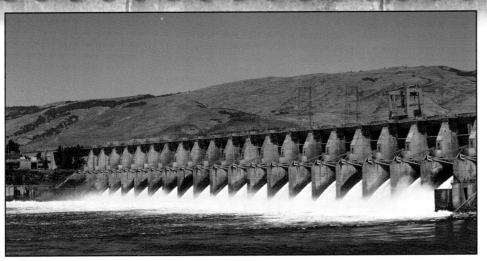

Strengthening side-parts called buttresses means that the main wall at this dam in Oregon, USA can be quite thin.

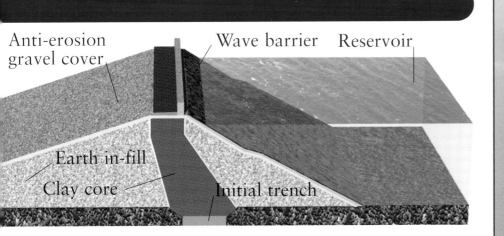

Anti-erosion gravel cover

Wave barrier   Reservoir

Earth in-fill

Clay core

Initial trench

WHERE ARE DAMS BUILT?

A dam is usually built across a river's narrow section, with high banks, as in a canyon or gorge. This uses fewer materials. The low areas behind the dam fill to form a lake or reservoir. Planners must take care that this does not flood whole cities!

Tarbela Dam in northern Pakistan is the largest earth-filled embankment design. It is part of a huge scheme along the mighty Indus River.

Green ISSUES

The reservoir behind a dam floods a vast area. This may be rich in ancient monuments, farms, wildlife and other precious sites. In rare cases, whole villages and even very rare animals are moved, to escape the relentless rise of the water.

A reservoir during a drought reveals an old hedgerow.

The Colorado River's Hoover Dam, USA, has a bowl-like double-curve to resist pressure.

HYDROELECTRIC DAM

Power from waterwheels is only available right next to the river. But a hydroelectric power station changes the force of moving water into our favourite form of energy – electricity. This electrical power can be sent great distances along wires.

In times of flood, spillways allow the extra water through the dam and along the original river.

THE HYDROELECTRIC DAM AND POWER STATION

The dam holds back water to form a reservoir. The deeper the reservoir, the greater the water pressure at its base. This water blasts along tunnels under the main dam, to spin the turbines in the power station (see page 17). The reservoir has enough water stored 'in reserve' so that the power station can keep generating even in times of drought.

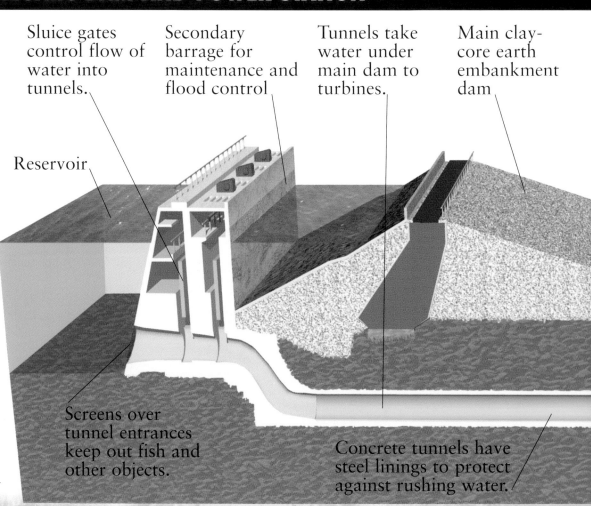

Sluice gates control flow of water into tunnels.

Secondary barrage for maintenance and flood control

Tunnels take water under main dam to turbines.

Main clay-core earth embankment dam

Reservoir

Screens over tunnel entrances keep out fish and other objects.

Concrete tunnels have steel linings to protect against rushing water.

Hydroelectricity means 'water electricity'. It uses the energy of moving water, which came originally from the Sun's warmth. The water's motion is harnessed by turbines and changed by generators into electrical energy (see next page). From Norway to New Zealand, places with many fast-flowing rivers can make more than nine-tenths of their electricity in this way.

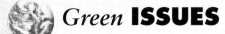

Green ISSUES

Many fish, seals, dolphins and other animals travel along rivers on migration, to breed. Dams block their way. A row of small waterfalls and channels, the 'fish ladder', helps them get past.

Salmon leap natural falls.

Control room staff check the turbines and generators, and match their electrical output with demand.

Tunnels taper to speed up water flow.

Transformers

Control rooms

Electricity flows away.

Generators

Water flows away along river bed.

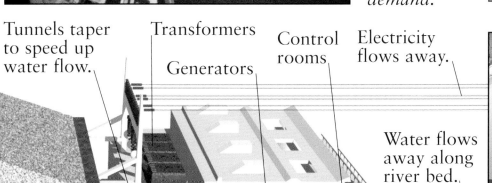

Rushing water spins turbines.

Row of generator-turbines

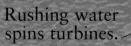

Hydroelectricity is not made from water itself. It comes from the energy of moving water. After water gives up some of its energy, it flows on to the sea, to continue its part in the water cycle. So hydroelectricity is a long-term, sustainable form of energy.

TURBINES

The key parts of the hydroelectric power station are the dam (see previous page), turbines and generators. Turbines are huge machines, with angled blades on a central shaft that can spin around.

Overhead power lines on pylons carry electricity away, above the Dallas Dam hydroelectric power station.

Green ISSUES

A hydroelectric power station is one of the cleanest ways to make electricity. It does not burn precious fossil fuel, which would produce air pollution and greenhouse gases. A drawback is the effects of the dam. It floods land upstream, reduces water flow downstream, and interferes with wildlife.

TURBINE TYPES

There are several designs of turbine, with different shapes and layouts of the blades, shaft and casing. Each design obtains the most energy from water flowing at a particular speed and pressure. The impulse wheel version is similar to the traditional waterwheel.

Kaplan axial flow turbine (upright shaft)

Pelton impulse wheel turbine

GENERATORS

The power of water pushes the blades and spins them on their shaft, in the same way that moving air – wind – turns a windmill. Also on the shaft is the generator, found in most kinds of power stations. It turns the energy of rotating motion into electrical energy. Usually one turbine spins one generator on the same shaft. Some power stations have several turbines linked by gears to one generator.

Fossil fuels cause air pollution.

THE GENERATOR

Generators work by electromagnetic induction – when a magnet moves past a wire, electricity flows in the wire. The magnetism is created by electro-magnets, where electricity flows through the rotating wire coils of the rotor. Much more electricity is created in the stationary wire coils of the stator around the rotor.

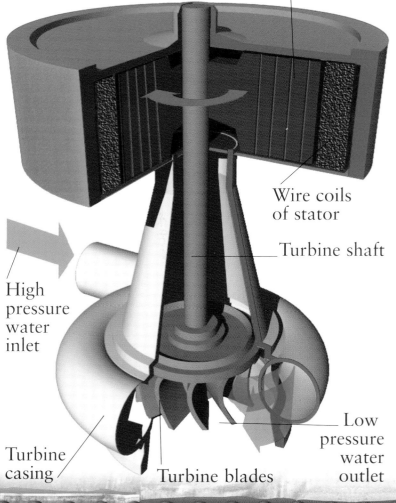

Electromagnet wire coils of rotor

Wire coils of stator

Turbine shaft

High pressure water inlet

Low pressure water outlet

Turbine casing

Turbine blades

Electricity from the generator is altered by transformers. These give it more force, or voltage, to travel along power lines.

17

Water is so important in today's world, that it is rarely used as an energy source alone. Hydroelectric schemes, with their dams and power stations, are usually combined with plans for other uses of water.

In west India, the Narmada River project includes one of the world's largest concrete dams. This holds back water during the monsoon (rains), which would otherwise flood large areas.

ON THE FARM

One of water's most precious uses, especially in dry areas, is for irrigation, to grow farm crops such as rice. Water is stored in the reservoir during the wet season, and let out gradually into nearby fields during the dry season, for the plants and also farm animals.

PUMPED STORAGE

Surge tunnel

Lower reservoir

Upper reservoir

Turbines

Upper pumping station

Lower pumping station

Our use of electricity varies through the day and year – for example, we use more on a cold evening. In pumped storage, when demand is high, water flows down from the upper reservoir to generate electricity, as usual. When demand is low, pumps use 'spare' electricity from the network to send the water back up again.

The biggest single water scheme is the Yangtze River Three Gorges project, China. The main dam, 183 metres high and 2.3 kilometres long, will have 26 giant turbines.

Farmland in south-central Argentina suffered a common problem – sudden heavy rain, then a long drought. The Cerros Colorados Dam stores the water to give a more even, year-round flow. Its power station supplies the city of Buenos Aires more than 1,000 kilometres away.

IN THE CITY

Water is vital in modern life for many reasons – drinking, cooking, washing, cleaning and flushing the toilet. In a developed country, each person uses more than 100 litres daily. Huge cities need vast supplies which come from dam reservoirs.

Green ISSUES

All plants need water, and the world's main food crops need more than most. If rains fail, water from a reservoir can be let through sluice gates into field channels, to soak into the soil. This causes fewer problems than pumping it up, from underground.

Lush greenery all year.

19

WATER NEEDS ENERGY!

Water is a source of energy – and it also uses up energy. It is collected, filtered, made clean and safe, and pumped along pipes, before it comes out of our taps. All these processes need supplies of electricity and other forms of energy, machines and raw materials. Water is big business!

JOBS IN WATER

Millions of people work in the water business. As well as dams and hydroelectric power stations, there are also purification plants, water treatment works, pumping stations, storage towers, and millions of kilometres of pipes and tubes under our cities and countryside.

Industries such as paper-making (top) and farming (above) use far more water than ordinary homes, offices and schools. In factories, water is used to clean, dissolve, lubricate (like oil), and as a coolant to carry away heat.

Waste water must be treated to remove germs and poisons. The leftovers can be dried and spread on the land as fertilizer.

Ancient TECHNOLOGY

The people of ancient Rome, over 2,000 years ago, understood the need for pure water which did not carry germs and spread diseases. They built long channels to bring clean water from remote areas flowing into their cities, bridging valleys with high aqueducts.

Pont du Gard aqueduct, southern France.

WAYS OF DE-SALTING

In reverse osmosis (below) sea water is pumped through a membrane. This lets fresh water through and holds back the salty minerals. In evaporation (bottom), the Sun's heat turns the water to vapour, leaving behind the salts, and the vapour is condensed.

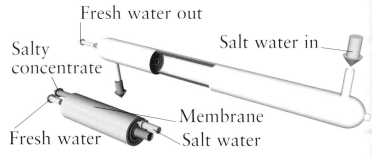

Fresh water out

Salt water in

Salty concentrate

Membrane

Fresh water

Salt water

FRESH WATER FROM SALTY

Some places suffer lack of water, even though huge amounts are a stone's throw away. These are desert areas by the sea. But sea water is salty and no use for drinking or cooking. Desalination (de-salting) uses energy to get rid of the salt and leave pure water.

Desalination towers cool vapour into water.

21

Energy can be added to water, to produce a powerful force which is useful in many ways, such as to move engines and vehicles. This added energy is heat, and the force is steam.

In the late 1800s, steam tractors and traction engines replaced farm horses – but diesel engines replaced them.

START THE REVOLUTION

Steam was vital for the Industrial Revolution of the 1700s. Steam engines powered newly invented machines as factories, industries and mass production spread around the world. In the 1800s the same happened with steam power on wheels, as railways spread. But steam engines waste much energy as lost heat. Petrol and diesel engines and electric motors took over. Today, natural steam generates electricity.

Wairakei geothermal power plant, one of the world's largest, supplies one-twentieth of New Zealand's electricity.

The energy of a geyser's spurting hot water and steam come from deep in the ground.

Places with natural hot springs, geysers, or red-hot rocks near the surface, have a free supply of geothermal or 'ground-heat' energy. This can be used directly in the area, to warm homes, schools and public places. Or it can be converted to electricity and transported long distances.

Geothermal trap, France.

GEOTHERMAL POWER

Cool water is pumped down into cracks in the rocks (1). Far below, the rocks are much hotter than at the surface (2). The water is heated under the pressure of great depth, and begins to boil (3). The steam and vapours rise up through cracks in the rocks and are gathered by pipes into the power station (4).

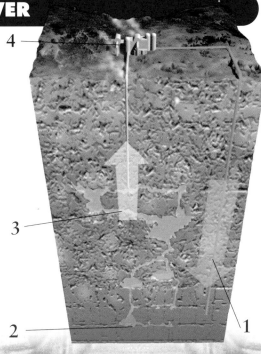

EARTH'S HEAT

Deep in the Earth, rocks are very hot – as we see when a volcano erupts. A geothermal power station traps super-hot water or steam rising from these layers, to spin turbines. But only a few places have hot rocks near the surface, for this to be useful.

A car engine uses up petrol or diesel (a limited resource), wastes energy as heat, and gives off many harmful exhaust fumes. An alternative is the fuel cell. It uses up hydrogen, which can be made from water. Its exhaust is water, too. It makes electricity to power a quiet, efficient motor. But fuel-cell cars are many years away.

Green ISSUES

Exhaust fumes from vehicle engines contain carbon dioxide and other 'greenhouse gases'. They also release poisonous carbon monoxide, and a mix of chemicals that worsen pollution problems such as acid rain and choking smog.

Pollution in Los Angeles.

Several car-makers are testing NE or 'no emission' vehicles. These do not spew out dangerous gases and vapours from their exhausts, which build up in areas with heavy traffic, to cause breathing and other health problems.

NE is especially important in cities, with many traffic jams and stop-start driving. Even when a petrol or diesel vehicle is still, its engine still runs and gives out exhaust fumes.

NE-cars are designed to test how fuel cells work on the road.

RUNNING ON WATER

A fuel cell has few moving parts. It works by adding hydrogen gas fuel to the oxygen gas in air. The result is water, released as a vapour, plus energy, which is in the form of electricity, to drive a motor.

But problems include how to make, transport and store hydrogen. It can be made by splitting water into hydrogen and oxygen gases but this, in turn, uses up electricity. Also hydrogen gas, even when squashed under great pressure, takes up huge amounts of space.

Spare fuel recycled

Exhaust water vapour

Electrode (positive)

Electrode (negative)

Central electrolyte membrane

Fuel flow plate

Air flow plate

Air in

Hydrogen fuel in

Electric current to/from motor

Electricity powers motor.

Future fuel-cell car – quiet, clean, efficient?

HOW FUEL CELLS WORK

A fuel cell is like a hydrogen-powered battery. Hydrogen fuel flows though one side, while air containing oxygen flows through the other. A central sheet, the electrolyte membrane, allows the two gases to combine and release the tiny bits of atoms called electrons. These can only move one way, so the process sets up a regular flow of electrons – which is an electric current.

25

WAVE POWER

Any form of moving water has energy. This includes waves, which are caused by winds blowing over the sea's surface. Winds, in turn, are caused by the Sun. It heats air, which rises, and cooler air blows along to take its place. So the energy of waves, like the energy in a flowing river, came originally from the Sun.

DIFFICULT TO HARNESS

A river with a dam provides a continuous, smooth flow of energy, to convert into electricity. Wave energy is extreme and unpredictable. Days of calm may be followed by a gale with giant breakers. Wave power is sustainable, pollution-free and has little effect on the environment, but harnessing its varied and violent nature is a great challenge for designers and engineers.

Large, curved, floating slabs called 'nodding ducks' tilt to and fro as waves pass. Their motions, like any physical movement, can be used by a generator to make electricity. The duck design helps to smooth out the most extreme surges of water.

Problems, **PROBLEMS**

A storm creates massive waves, taller than houses, which crash down with rock-shattering force. They have damaged several test-design wave generators. Also, salt water quickly eats away at materials such as metals.

A big wave contains hundreds of tonnes of water.

SHORELINE DESIGN

The shoreline generator traps the alternate rise and fall of a wave's water level. The motion blows and then sucks air, like a bicycle pump, through an air turbine. This spins the propeller-like blades inside, which are connected to a generator. The shoreline design can be useful on remote islands, but the rise and fall of tides limits its reliability.

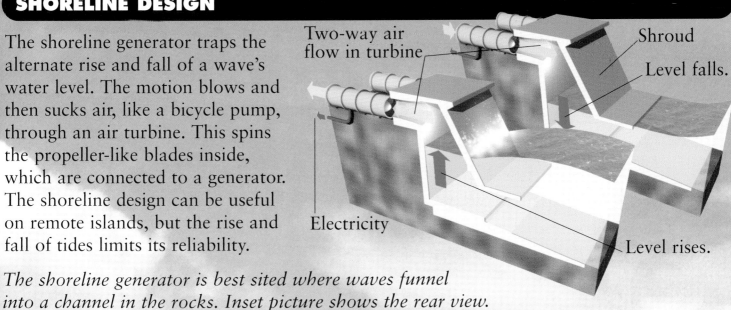

Two-way air flow in turbine

Shroud

Level falls.

Electricity

Level rises.

The shoreline generator is best sited where waves funnel into a channel in the rocks. Inset picture shows the rear view.

TIDAL POWER

More steady and regular than wave energy (see previous page) is the relentless rise and fall of the tide. Tidal power is another way to harness the energy of moving water for electricity.

TWO-WAY FLOW

As the sea level rises with an incoming tide, water moves from the ocean into the mouth or estuary of a river. The tide passes, the level falls and the river water resumes its journey into the sea. The water flow caused by these changing levels is like a two-way river and can generate electricity. But there are risks of storm damage and environmental effects.

HOW TIDES HAPPEN

The forces of gravity from the Moon and Sun create tides. The Moon pulls a bulge of water on the part of the Earth nearest to it. As the Earth spins, once each day, this bulge travels around it. With the Sun and Moon at right angles, their gravities act against each other to give neap tides, with a small range. With the Moon and Sun in line, their gravities add to give extra-high, extra-low spring tides.

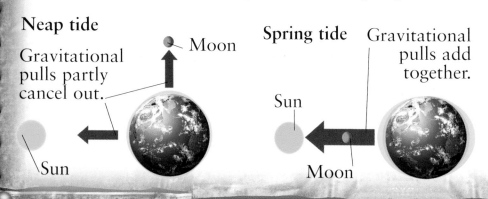

Neap tide

Gravitational pulls partly cancel out.

Moon

Sun

Spring tide

Gravitational pulls add together.

Sun

Moon

THE TIDAL BARRAGE

The tidal barrage is like a hydroelectric dam across a river, with turbines and generators. As the tide falls, the water flow from river to sea builds up to a peak over three hours, then slows over the next three hours. It then repeats the process as the tide rises, but in the other direction. The barrage is also a useful bridge linking the two banks of the estuary. A gap with a tilting roadway allows boats to pass.

Annapolis Royal, Nova Scotia, Canada and La Rance, France (below) are the only two working tidal barrages in the world.

Green ISSUES

A tidal barrage smooths out water level changes along the banks of the river and nearby coast. This affects shore animals such as fish, crabs and shellfish, and wading birds who probe the mud for worms and other food.

Crabs greet a rising tide.

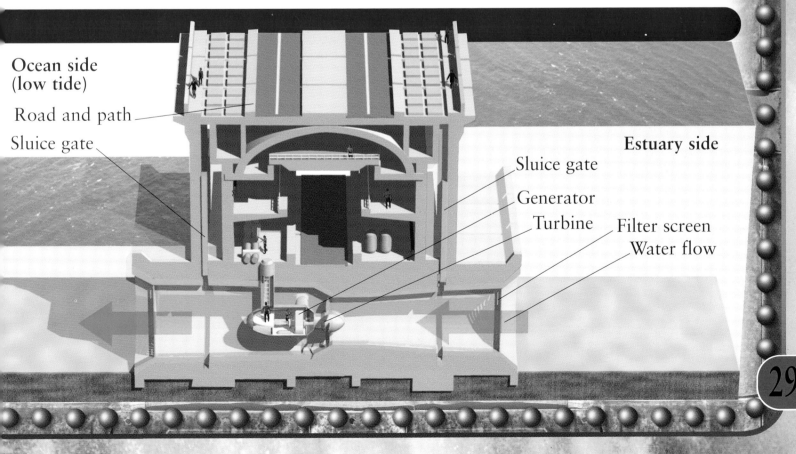

Ocean side (low tide)

Road and path

Sluice gate

Estuary side

Sluice gate

Generator

Turbine

Filter screen

Water flow

As we use up coal, oil and other fossil fuels, can water provide energy for our future needs? There is a limit on rivers to dam for hydroelectricity, so other methods must be explored.

ULTIMATE ENERGY?

Winds and water currents are both created by the Sun's warmth. But wind power is dwarfed by the massive flow of ocean currents, called gyres. Trapping the energy in their motion is a gigantic task for engineers. But it could produce vast amounts of 'clean, green' electricity in years to come.

THERMAL GIANT

Ocean depths are much colder than the surface. If sea bed water was bubbled up by gas, its difference in temperature from surface water could be tapped, by a heat-exchanger device, to spin turbines.

Warm surface water

Turbines and generators

Heat exchanger

Cold sea bed water

Gas flow down

Cold water flow up

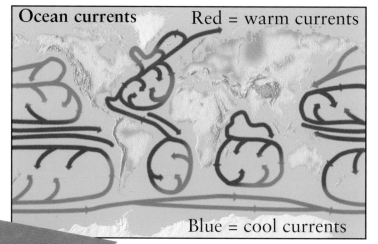

Ocean currents — Red = warm currents

Blue = cool currents

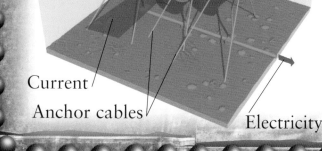

Underwater turbines

Current

Anchor cables

Electricity

CURRENT TURBINES

Turbines similar to those in hydroelectric power stations could be placed underwater, in regions with powerful, steady ocean currents. However, the great water pressure and the corrosion effect of salt water are just two of the many problems.

GLOSSARY

dissolve
Spread as tiny particles through a liquid called the solvent (see right). A dissolved substance seems to disappear, but it is still there.

estuary
The mouth or end of a river, as it widens and flows into the sea.

evaporate
Change from a liquid into a gas or vapour. As water evaporates from a puddle, we call it 'drying'.

global warming
The rise in temperature all around the world, due to greenhouse gases (see below) in the layer of air, or atmosphere. They trap extra amounts of the Sun's heat.

greenhouse gases
Substances in the atmosphere (air) which hold in or retain the Sun's heat. They keep it near to Earth's surface, rather than letting it escape into space, causing global warming (see above).

purification
Making a substance pure, so that only it is present, and nothing else, by taking out all other substances.

solvent
The liquid that a substance dissolves in or spreads through (see left). When sugar dissolves in water, the solvent is water.

sustainable
A process or substance that can continue for a very long time, and will not run out, be used up or wear away.

turbine
A shaft (central rod or axle) with a circle of angled blades, like a fan. These spin around when steam or another high-pressure substance blows past them.

vapour
A substance which is in the form of a gas, rather than a liquid or solid, and which can be turned into a liquid by cooling.